BORN BACKWARDS

BORN BACKWARDS

POEMS

TANYA OLSON

YESYES BOOKS | PORTLAND

COVER & INTERIOR DESIGN: ALBAN FISCHER
PROJECT LEAD: KMA SULLIVAN
AUTHOR PHOTO CREDIT: ADRIANNE MATHIOWETZ

ISBN 978-1-936919-99-4
PRINTED IN THE UNITED STATES OF AMERICA

PUBLISHED BY YESYES BOOKS
1631 NE BROADWAY ST #121
PORTLAND, OR 97232
YESYESBOOKS.COM

KMA SULLIVAN, PUBLISHER
DEVIN DEVINE, ASSISTANT EDITOR
ALBAN FISCHER, GRAPHIC DESIGNER
KARAH KEMMERLY, MANAGING EDITOR
JILL KOLONGOWSKI, MANUSCRIPT COPY EDITOR
JAMES SULLIVAN, ASSISTANT EDITOR
GALE MARIE THOMPSON, SENIOR EDITOR, BOOK DEVELOPMENT

For these knots in my string

Edna L (Utter) Harn February 10 1907 – October 14 1980

Beulah Mae (Utter) Ogden January 30 1925 – December 12 2005

Edith Irene (Utter) Ward March 10 1919 – August 30 1975

Mildred Ann (Campbell) Olson December 5 1943 – September 20 1995

CONTENTS

He is dead who called me into being; and when I shall be no more, the very remembrance of us both will speedily vanish.

Frankenstein. MARY SHELLEY

Nature held me close and seemed to find no fault with me.

Stone Butch Blues. LESLIE FEINBERG

There are the ones who do see me see me there are the ones who do see me see me there are the ones who do who do see me there are the ones who do see me.

How To Write. GERTRUDE STEIN

BORN BACKWARDS

Feet first Ready to run
Problem for the doctor
Danger to my mother
Forceps lock around
my skull Three firm tugs
leave a permanent dent
Such the queer
way to begin

An early reader My first job
to toddle down the driveway
Fetch the paper Read
headlines aloud *White House
Defends Air Raids Farm Prices
Recover* Never learned to read
Just read A skill already
inside me Games on the way
to see Grandma Spell
what we see *P-I-G pig
C-O-W cow D-O-N-K-E-Y
donkey* What we hear on the radio
*That's Elvis E-L-V-I-S They say
he's back but he never really
went away*

I stay with Grandma for a week
at the beginning and end

of each summer Jobs at home
don't have a name but
Grandma calls them chores
Feed sheep Weed beds Pick beans
You get the low ones I'll get the high
Together we make a perfect pair
These summer visits the purest
love I ever know Fertile seeds
in hungry soil

At lunch the radio plays
funeral music Deep voice
Service place and time Grandma
tells me something about each
name we hear Kin Job Where
she saw them last We nap
and wake to watch *General Hospital*
which I always think is *The Doctors*
because of the way it starts
When the party line rings not our ring
Grandma turns down the sound
Raises her eyebrows Puts a finger
to her lips Picks up and listens
long enough to know what she
needs to know

Before bed I read to her
from a chapter book She buys
them for me from yard sales
Saves them when the library
throws them out This one

describes how a dairy runs
When I correctly pronounce
pasteurize Grandma shakes
her head in awe *How could*
a little girl even know that word
Sometimes I swear you must
have lived before

While I am away
the yellow apple tree
at home is split in two
by lightning My father
builds a stand in its still
living half *For you For reading*
High enough I can gaze
over the corn Having never
seen an ocean I imagine I am
a sailor lost at sea From my nest
I work through a stack
of Great Kid Classics Up there
I eat the apples that continue
to grow at hand Buried in each
lies the tang of fire

One songy poem roots in me
that summer A caught fish
turns into a woman and promptly
runs away That summer I live
off the ground Beneath the sky
Surrounded by the rustle
of tall-as-me corn Below

the constant thrum of wasps
drunk on windfall apples
Every morning I battle
Roo the meanest rooster
who ever lived His flash
of spurs when I gather eggs
hurts my feelings *All Roo knows*
is to protect the flock
my mother counsels *And to him*
you are just a giant girl who steals

Chores for Grandma are gentler
Feed the bottle lambs Give them
names But lambs can frighten too
Such hunger when they spot me
carrying the milk bucket The power
the need in their unrelenting suck
Before she opens the pasture gate
Grandma rubberbands bread bags
over my shoes As she makes supper
Grandma ties a string to each end
of the flyswatter so I can wear it
over my shoulder Play it like a guitar
She claps every time I spin around
and announce *Hello My name*
is Johnny Cash

When my parents come to take me
back I introduce them to the lambs
Share the names I have chosen

Peanuts Popcorn CrackerJack
My mother feeds them apple slices
while they gently lip her hand

My friend Clark insists
the only people who want
big gardens as adults
never worked in one
as kids He is not entirely
wrong about this Every day
requires something
Hoe Dig Plant Weed Water Pick
My least favorite job
is plucking hornworms
off the tomatoes I drown each
in a coffee can of kerosene I later
use to light the trash barrel fire
Sing to each as they go *Return*
to sender Address unknown
Lay down amid the corn
to hide and read *Frankenstein*

The monster learns to fit in
by watching others The monster
runs so as not to hurt what he loves
The monster promises *I will be*
with you on your wedding night
The monster does not believe
himself a monster but the world
will not agree

The contentment of that summer
does not last Soon I begin to dream
of leaving Believe to really be
I must be somewhere else
Clothes Jobs Books Music
the ways I build this distance

I still love Elvis Still read
voraciously Grow only
tomatoes Name animals
thematically This year
my dentist correctly
identified me as a wellwater kid
No fluoride in those early years
makes the teeth you have today

I always misremember
how that fish poem ends The woman
gets away but the man vows
to find her and keep her
until time and times are done
Some book taught me
I was different from my parents
Some book told me
queer kids run

DON'T COME HOME

she said Don't bring home
she said To me she said
who you are is impossible

Words like seeds root
in unintended places
Corn amid the beans
Volunteers Wrong field

In me the tendril rooted
In me tendrils spread like a bruise

The worst thing she said is not
the most important thing about
her Hurt is not what I remember

Instead I imagine she was
trying to say Life is already
hard Why choose something
to make it harder

Death is most terrible as
the end of a chance to change

Given more time we could have
plowed that moment under
Could have planted it again

Come home she would say
Bring home she would say
To me she would say your life
is a bountiful field of possible

To me there is nothing
you can not do

READER LAST NIGHT

I dreamt you I laid down
my poethead to dream
my poetdreams

My father dreamt
of answers Keys
locked in the car
Woke knowing where
to lower the coathanger
What to catch How to lift
Saw it like an X-ray
The door and its insides

My mother dreamt
of people Her dead
and other folks she
wished she could see
We were having
such a good visit
I hated to wake up

Me reader I dreamt
of you You my absent
You my answer
Watched you like
a movie One person

after another reading
a book not yet writ

From the front seat
10 minutes to shift
Spine cracked open
Book left behind
to ride shotgun

In a laundromat with
a fierce concentration
Book held open
by the basket Eyes
on words while hands
fold clothes

By a young girl in a tree
Around her corn
rustles in the golden
breeze She holds
the book in one hand
In the other a yellow
apple plucked from the tree
Gnawed straight
through Inside her
seeds of fire take root
and sprout

I wake and write down
Not in order
Not in one sitting

Of course not
I understand
Ours is a time
made of nothing
but fits and starts

Still more people
visit a library
every year than go
to the movies And why not
Movies are expensive
and terrible All comic strips
and tortured women
Where is the movie
featuring the tired old lesbian
who suffers hot flashes
The butch who falls in love
with her own anger
Call me when you make those
Otherwise I will stick
with books

Read this as you will then
Not like school Not like
a riddle For these
are your poems and you
are their people And they
are so glad to see you again

WHAT A POEM DO

is what anything made do Make
the maker Build a world When
AP went to the valley to catch
songs Sara fell in love

with Coy Coy of the bluest
eyes Coy what stayed
to the mountain Coy
who kept the fields AP

was meant to tend Makers
work to make then abandon
what gets made When the Carter
Family started to get played

on the radio his mother took
Coy to California Got him
away from those Carters Makers
often resent both the making

and the what gets made Sara
knew what her deep alto cost
her Sara knew what a radio
do Years later on XERA

a Mexican border blaster
sitting on the Texas line Sara
stepped to the mike and sang
the most successful song

ever writ *I am thinking*
tonight of my blue eyes
And I wonder if he ever
thinks of me In California

Coy was listening as he always
listened Turned to his mother
and said *I reckon I ought*
to go get her His mother agreed

I reckon I guess you ought
Same mother what took him
from her in the first place
Same mother who hid every letter

one sent to the other Who
understands a mother Who
understands her ever shifting
heart Mothers are makers

who shear apart what is made
so to stitch it together again
Coy drove to Texas where he
and Sara married Sara left

13

her children Sara left Clinch Mountain
Sara left music for 30 years
until she and Maybelle reunited
on *The Johnny Cash Show*

and sang *You are my flower*
that's blooming in the mountain
for me You are my flower
that's blooming there for me An old

old song no one knows who wrote
No one alive knows who Sara sang
to the night she sang again in public
And that *you* is what a poem do

WHY WE INVENTED

the radio was because
   of the dead Dead is because
      of the wars Wars is always
         a question of nation Nation

question come down to
   Who is Human Who is
      Human is no legitimate
         question to ask Who is

human is anyone who try
   to talk to their dead Why
      a desire to talk to the dead
         Talk to the dead for guidance

and wisdom Belief that the
   dead hold deeper knowledge
      Have an angle on the world
         we living just do not see Talk

to the dead to remember
   Talk to the dead so to ask
      questions forgot to ask when
         alive Where did you when did

you Why in the world did
     we do it that way Answers
          heard not lost Answers heard
               never forgot Believe in the dead

because Germs Telegraph
     Telephone Photograph Radio
          Can't see them work But there
               they are Can't see them But they

crawl inside you Get in your
     ear Get in your eye Before
          these were invented dead
               tap tap tap Take someone else

to say what the tap tap mean
     Before these things dead enter
          another body Use that mouth
               to say what they want to the alive

After these things you hear
     the dead your ownself See
          them on your own Shadow
               in a picture Voice inside the

static Now living got direct
     access to those in between
          Edison believe the whispers
               of the dead always around us

He invent a Spirit Phone so as
   to hear them Hear from Jesus
     if Jesus feel like talking that day
      Hear what your mother think about

you now Marconi think anything
   ever said still a wave somewhere
     in this universe His Spirit Radio way
      way to find it and hear it Hear the last

words of Christ as he dying on
   the cross Hear what your mother
     whisper in your ear the first time
      you met Some folks believe dead

live in between the stations Dead
   the broadcaster Radio and TV right
     kind of receiver Spicer say the poet
      a certain type of radio Poet got a kind

of antenna Tune in to a frequency
   Listen close Write it down Spicer
     say poet got to learn to hear it accurate
      Spicer say poet have to write it automatic

POET IS PIG

born in a barn Pig pregnant
3 months 3 weeks 3 days
Day 4 Come a pig Most pig
born tuck in their hooves Slide
out headfirst Special pig
born backwards Poem arrive
any which way Poet push
pen on paper Push Push
Come a poem Make the poem
You a poet Pretty poem Pretty
pig Squeal pig Waller pig
Piggy having roast beef Piggy
having none Creep feed Wean
pig Farrow barn to nursery

Farm life the soft life Straight
shot from born to die No
sunburn danger No coyote
harm Heat lamp Vent fan
Farmer play the oldies station
all summer long Why pig love
a line dance Like poet love a line
dance Pig don't sweat like poet
don't sweat Time release
trough feed one pen
at a time Stand there Wait
your turn Lazy pig Porky pig

Eating order the only thing
poet or pig gonna fight about

Pig walk itself to finishing barn
Corn Soybean Vitamin Mineral
16 weeks later Big P Pig
Don't every pig make it Lady pig
Lesbian pig Pig of a certain age
Eloise told me *You can knock*
and knock at poetry's frontdoor
but you will never get in that way
Eloise told me *The lesbian poet*
dies and they gather to anoint
another It is never going
to be someone like you It will
never be a woman like me

Don't everyone end up some
Big P Poet Pig stay on the farm
get shot stuck scalded gutted
Pigman use every scrap of pig
there is *Rooter to the tooter*
my mother like to say *Even*
try to save the squeal Pigman
pile up the heads Make what
he call cheese In it you can see
the shadow of little pig ears
In it you see they little snouts

Pig in the wild called Boar
Hair wear to tough like steel

Teeth grow out to tusk Tusk
made good to dig Tusk made
good for gash Out here we eat
what we want Out here we find
what we eat Out here we write
as we will Out here we gather
every night and sing *I ain't young*
nor pretty No twinkle in my eye
If I don't work I'll starve to death
Root hog or die

KARMA POLICE

is a song by Radiohead whose first two words
repeat the title First Karma Then Police

My cats would write this KarMuh Poleez
and RayDeeOHed but have yet to find a reason to

They leave notes Fead Uz and sign cards
Hapee BurdDay Humee but are not big fans of Radiohead

Too pretentious they say *Too thinky Too sad*
Cats may spell erratically but they speak accurately

Cats are lovers of dance and find
the think interferes with the rhythm

I explain the times to defend the song *Everyday*
was a War on Something Day after day of impossible war

Or maybe then I thought anything complex was better
Fancy over simple is a common sin of youth

You can't swing the music too much the other way though
Put on the Carter Family and the cats complain about that too

Enuf Enuf Uv Dis HillBilEe Pluck reads the note
they stick to *The Storms Are On The Ocean*

When I play that album I think of my mother listening to it
imagining her family hearing the same song without her

I'm going away to leave you love
I'm going away for awhile

That vision made a stone in her
she could never learn to swallow around

The cats do like some '90s songs PryVut Ayez and Werk Dat
are scrawled under Pawzubl Toonz 4 Grate CatPartees

Cats organize by list and title Cats laugh
at the idea dinosaurs became birds

Cats live in a culture parallel to our own
A different society that uses our infrastructure

Smaller scooters drive on our roads Libraries
hold hidden stacks full of Great Cat Books

Different cat music Separate cat money
Cats think *trousers* is our funniest word

What if there are no karma chameleons
What if there is no karma police

What if life is a random string of things that happen
What if cats don't even know how to write

What if no cats dance or throw all night parties
Maybe cats can not talk or hold jobs or drive

What if their sass their plans their poems
are the way I built to best talk to myself

No cat union No cat symphony
Wut IvItt Awl Wuz Ownlee Me

BURD N DA MOWTH

kary songz n itz mowth

Burd songz n itz mowth
    n da mowth
        uv da katt

Katt holt da burd Duznt kloz Duznt kyl
Katt karyz burd to spen tym wit duh ded

Katt wizpurr to itz pray
az it layz in da mowth

Iz OK litul sparrow
Iz OK litul mows
I iz redee wen u redee
Wen u redee u kin go

Den da katt dropz da burd
    dropz da fedders
        dropz da beek

Den da katt keepz da songz
    uv da burd
        n itz mowf

than receiver my father taught
me much Happy to instruct
Less interested in learn To hunt
his first lesson for me Not deer
Not squirrel *Too much walking*
I leave too early You are too
young You are too loud But birds
Fields and waterways around
the house Late afternoons
Early fall

      Doves No sons
No hunting dogs Just me
Flush he calls Squatting
where corn meets beans
Wearing their dead brown
for camouflage *Flush*
My cue to walk to him
through stubble the birds
glean until we disc it under
There chaff sleeps and rots
to feed what comes next

            Corn
surrounds us one year Beans
around us the next We do not
eat what grows in the field

Commodity crops Feedlot
corn for cows that prefer
grazing Converted into mash
made to swell up a hog
Every season some corn
pops up in the beans Some
beans sprout amid the corn
Seed that roots in the wrong
field called a volunteer As if
it asked to be different As if
it wanted to be alone
Chopped down Uprooted
when big enough So as not
to shade what grows
under them So they have no
access to nutrients not meant
for them

      The night before
we practice raising birds
Doves flee from motion
not sound So walk Jump
Wave your arms Be sure
you spook them east Fly
them out of the sun I gallop
down the row Whirl my hands
to say away Their sudden their
startle more than I imagined
The gun fluid in its rise carves
the sky Gun to shoulder Cheek
to stock Barrel ahead to cover

the quarry Bang and Bang *Keep*
your eyes on where they fall
Otherwise we might never
find them Small ones are easy
to lose I run right to the fallen
First dead Second winged I jam
its head between my fingers
Thumb the head still Twist Pull
Just like we practiced on grapes
that morning Bleed them out
Dress them in the field Eat
the breasts for supper Hearts
kept frozen for year end

Later

in the season pheasants My father
upwind while I walk the waterway
Afternoon into dark Cold into colder
His blaze orange cap atop my head
To keep you warm So I can spot you
in the field Pheasants he teaches
prefer walk to fly The dead grass
parts as I drive a pair ahead of me
I walk when they walk I run when
they run We bust cover together
Pheasants are big enough for
the slap of a shotgun Big enough
we always see where he falls
We only kill one We only kill boys
Know them by their ringneck
Know them by their tailfeathers

The 12-gauge pump means they tend
not to be alive when we find them
What do we do if he is My father
touches the knife he wears at his side
and places the pheasant inside
the game bag my mother sewed
to the back of my vest I feel his dying
heat against me the cold walk home
Dressing him later my father hands me
the longest tailfeather for my ballcap
Shows me how to wedge the quill
between the backsnaps so it sticks
straight up So colorful So elegant
Now I'll know it's you from
a mile away

        My father teaches
me to drive I want to start with
the small tractor but the combine
is my favorite ridealong when he will
take me The high glass cockpit Its slow
sweep through the field How ahead
stands tall How behind lies down
Plead my case in the cab Back
pressed to the windshield Arm
propped atop the transistor Always
tuned to the local farm channel
Weather Markets End of day report
Live cattle Lean hog Corn Beans Futures
I explain I am big enough now
to be helpful Can do more than just

work in the garden More than only
gather eggs He agrees and lays out a plan
Pushmower Riding mower
Small tractor Farm truck Bean wagon
Car Grain wagon Big tractor Combine
I am not a child I know combine is ages
away But what can I do except agree
He drops me off the next row end turn
We start tomorrow I climb down
Defeated Determined

                  The pushmower
is Boring Heavy Loud First I learn
to fill and check the gas and oil
How to prime the engine How to pull
the rope He stresses the importance
of focus Points out the parts
that can maim That will hurt
Stop thinking for just one moment
and it's byebye fingers byebye toes
I cut the edges Small parts
the riding mower misses
or can not reach This is for
babies I am driving nothing
I am going nowhere Four mows
later Fingers and toes still attached
I graduate We review oil gas blades
He introduces brake clutch gears
I press the starter and promptly
crash into the side of the house
Did it jump out in front of you

he teases as I try not to cry Explain
how I did not expect the leap the roar
How its speed felt like panic
How the noise made it hard to think
You'll get used to it he promises
Until then let's keep the house
standing and practice over here
In the empty side pasture

                              I learn
to hit nothing To this day I still cut
my own grass Push mower through
suburban yard I came to love the quiet
its noise makes Value the bubble
inside its roar Sometimes I grouse
I bet Yeats never had to stop writing
to mow around the tower but sadder
him if it is true As the body walks
the mind is free to mull and ponder
Create new lines Rewrite the old
You have to learn to read the lay
of the land my father taught me
See the pattern Feel when it rises
Note where it falls On the turn
pivot on the inside backwheel
and drop the front tire in the track
you just made That way you end up
with smart straight lines

                    Mow your own
grass Clean your own home Else how
will you see the earth grow tired
How will you notice when
the birds take wing

A MOTHER DEEP

face down
  in the belly
    of her own

child *There*
  can be times
    my own human

mother assures
  me *it is better*
    this way If the

kitten will not
  suck If the other
    kittens turn on it

A quicker
  way Slightly
    more humane

Mother farm
  born Barn born
    A mother eager

to mother
  A mother
    eager to feast

MY DIORAMA GAME

was strong that summer Diorama
my chosen craft the week
of Vacation Bible School A craft
I refine over the school year
A year I never imagined could end

Begin by laying a shoebox
on its longside Draw backgrounds
on properly measured and trimmed
sheets of paper Tape the sheets
together and roll them between
2 toilet paper tubes attached
to the back of the box Glue the main
characters to the floor of the box
Time appears to pass for the viewer
as the drawing moves right to left
Add dialogue to drive the action
With a triggering event
the plot begins

Dinosaurs Cavemen Noah
No story too big that year
The setting always a flatland
Tree and Grass Sun and Sky
I knew nought of a mountain
Knew not of the sea
A brontosaurus eyes the flash

of the comet *Another beautiful*
sunrise Noah looks up *Starting*
to rain Caveman shivers *Brrrrrr*
under my darkening sky

Life on earth never sits static
Species and planets come
then they go Mass extinction
is when many species all die
together at once Coextinction
is when the disappearance
of one species triggers the loss
of the next Functional
extinction occurs when
there are so few of a species
reproduction becomes impossible
Planned extinction is all of anything
getting rounded up to be destroyed
A cantilean extinction happens
when a species goes missing before
it was even known to exist No species
has ever gone extinct by replacement
An endling is the final member
of a species left alive

Dioramas are the best medium
for stories of extinction Dioramas
are perfect for tales that draw
to a hard fast end Dioramas
a theater reliant upon illusion

The finest dioramas transport
viewers Effective dioramas violate
both space and time

The longest days on the ocean
occur when winds fail to blow
Those days there is naught
to look at but water Days sailors
believe come from a curse
The doldrums sailors call
such days Days that play
with the mind To pass them
sailors take to their berths
and make models of the ship
on which they sit stuck
Little men left
calm and windless
In a bottle In a box
On a box On the sea

VANITY FAIR

is an old philosophical term which refers to
the flawed world in which we live and its preference

for idle pleasures In *Pilgrim's Progress* Bunyan
makes it an actual place built by demons to distract

the faithful with *fools, apes, knaves, and rogues,*
and that of every kind Thackeray borrowed

the term to title his novel of corruption and greed
A novel that points out the cost inherent in trying

to become a person you are not *Vanity Fair* next
a magazine centered on culture and fashion

published in the 1900s A magazine I never knew
existed until k.d. lang appeared on its cover

lathered up and sprawled across
a barber chair getting a close shave

from Cindy Crawford k.d. lang
so suave so smooth in her pinstripe

suit and pompadour k.d. lang
who loved Patsy Cline so much

she believed herself a kind of
reincarnation naming her first band

the Reclines k.d. lang who moved
to Nashville and was roundly ignored

by almost everyone in town except
Loretta Lynn and Minnie Pearl

despite being a top-selling country artist
for two years running Despite the richness

of tone rising from those flawless pipes
Butch dyke was so unimaginable in 1980s

Nashville lang sold more than a million
albums but mostly remained unknown So she

announced she was a vegan and a lesbian
and took out to California a place with

its own style of country music where
she made a different kind of album In LA

she met Madonna who promptly announced
Elvis is alive and she is beautiful Someone

in her hometown painted *Eat Beef Dyke*
on the town sign but by summer '92 we all

sang *constant craving has always been*
which landed lang on the cover of *Vanity Fair*

straddled by Crawford a straight
edge gently pressed to her neck

Vanity Fair was originally published
for 20 years before the Great Depression

killed it off The magazine returned
from the dead in the 1980s

and is still around today Unextinction
is the act of bringing a species back when

previously it was gone These days lang
accepts lifetime achievement awards and

issues remixes of her earlier albums *The muse*
is eluding me she recently said *I am at peace*

with the fact I may be done lang claims
singing *Every Breath You Take* with Chaka

Khan is her favorite performance
ever and she has a point The two

sound amazing together but lang also admits
talking about her own career is akin to asking

an apple how it thinks it might taste *No apple*
lang insists *knows how it tastes* Reextinction

is the act of reviving a lost species just
to be able to kill it off again Our world

is but an island stocked with deceitful
wares Lord Old Man Lord Carnal Delight

huddle together to giggle and plot
and scheme It is easy enough to believe

yourself different Think you are but a pilgrim
merely wandering through Makers

know to dive in the pit if they wish
to disturb the trade Live bold

in the cage Razor firm to your throat
At the heart of our Vanity Fair

FACED WITH DEATH
MY MOTHER

i
cried for her own already dead
mother *Why won't she help me*
My mother knew ghosts Lived
with ghosts Talked with ghosts
She has to know I need her now
I know she would come if she could
What use ghosts How terrible
their absence

ii
My mother had only one
semester of college Came home
for Christmas Never went back
I liked my roommate The classes But
every night at supper I thought
about Mom Grandma Granddad
gathered at the table Radio playing
Me not there It made a lump
in my throat I simply could
never swallow around

iii
My mother the temper
of our family Threatened
when your dad gets home

but always handled it herself
She was the Spanker Yeller Thrower
of the two Flyswatter Wooden
spoon Whatever was at hand
But the lovingest one too
Hugged Asked Listened Supported
Bottomless throughout this life
In class one time a professor
asked us *Who here thinks*
hitting children is wrong
Everyone raised a hand *You may*
disappoint me my mother promised
but I will never not love you

iv
My mother spent her childhood
alone *Why I wanted two of you*
You will always have each other
Only child she sang to the sheep
Taught school to the chickens Lived
with her mother and grandparents
Father gone before she was born
Saw him once when I was five After
never again Took his red hair Loved
those who loved her Forgot those
who did not The professor asked us
Who here was spanked as a child
Almost everyone raised a hand again

v

My mother grew up on a farm No
electricity Outhouse until a teenager
Eventually found work in the city
Department of Motor Vehicles
Handling forms Sending out licenses
Her claim to fame Processed the paperwork
for Muhammad Ali when he changed
his name from Cassius Clay Quit
when she married my father
Already pregnant with me I like
that I was at the wedding Love
we looked alike sounded alike
Love we came into life alike Both
born bastard adjacent Later
back to school Cosmetology
Practiced on me *Lettucehead* they
called me in fourth grade All curls
and springs while she learned to perm
I never minded She worked tender
around my softspot dent That year
her hands always in my hair

vi

My mother believed cards
of the devil Didn't ban them
from the house But neither
were they present I finally
learned Hearts Spades playing
softball To pass the time on long
van rides Between games

Making bids Counting books
When Grandad was a boy
he and his brothers were meant
to be in the field Rain was coming
so they hid in the barn Second
hand dealt when lightning
struck Barn burnt down around
them They all escaped Idle hands
Devil's tool Those boys never
played cards again My mother
believed in saw ghosts UFOs Heard
barks and meows from pets long dead
Would talk about it if asked When I
left for college she hugged me and said
Don't bring home a black man Don't
come home gay I was never sure
if the professor's point was *And you*
came out OK or *Look how much*
you learned from the experience

vii
My mother was loved mourned missed
at her funeral Friends Family Colleagues
For her kindness For her caring
She worked harder than anyone
I will ever know Kept house
Cooked meals Had a giant garden
Canned it Pickled it Put it all up
Took vacation days for spring cleaning
Would ask about you Your family
Listened Followed up Was proud

of me My sister The family she built
Kept together No one mentioned
the office Everyone talked of her
compassion Her heart

viii
My mother read voraciously Loved
I read that way too Wanted to know
all I learned at college *It's called*
NPR I explained scanning the low
end of the dial *They just talk*
about the news all day long as someone
explained the UN doing or not doing
something *Boutros Boutros-Ghali*
she sang to a calypso beat as we entered
the store Granddaughter of farmers
Daughter of a lunchlady Chose my name
because she saw *Anna Karenina* After
she died I found a notebook Short stories
she wrote while sick Megan the central
character Who goes to college Writes
Travels What was your wildest dream
for yourself What would you have named
me if I was a boy These and other
questions I now only ask her ghost

ix
My mother died at home In bed A gift
of hospice I think she waited for me
to get there I said what every person
says in the ear of the dying *It's OK*

I said *We will be alright*
NPR on the radio *You can go*
I said At least she was not alone

x

My mother the age I am now
when she died I think what it might
mean to only have this much What
if this were my full life Wonder
what started what took her Well water
Chemicals in the beauty shop Cropdusters
and what they dropped The electric
fence Her favorite game as a child
Grab it See how long she could
hold on First one hand Then two
Dunked her hands in a bucket
of water Put one foot in the bucket
Then the other *I could take it* she laughed
explaining *I could just hold*
on and on Never enough sense
to let go

WE THE MENOPAUSAL

have a service to offer America A timely
service only we can offer A service
we can do best You see to be menopausal
is to be porous What is meant to stay in

leaks out Pee Hair Farts Words Grunts
Groans Thoughts On sitting On
standing While walking Access to what
others lock away is a superpower For to be

menopausal is to know how to erupt
Geothermal vent opens to a fiery molten core
Cooking from the inside how my mother
described hot flashes Menopausal

early like my mother I spend this year
trying not to die the same age
as my mother Eaten alive
while fires roiled inside her The *Hot-*

so-Hots Susan and I call them since
that is what we say when we throw off
the covers and flap the extra-loose
pajamas we bought since the flames

bloomed inside us Bedside fan Ceiling
fan oscillates all year round now Moods
swing back Swing forth More patient
than ever But also shorter

of temper For to be menopausal is
to be reversible Hot to cold Patient
to enraged No transition No clear
trigger Just the sudden flash Longer

vision Shorter fuse Depth Speed Fury
are the gifts of the menopausal Together
they offer the possibility of responsible
anger A service of focused hate An ability

to bring death to those for whom death
would only be an improvement A burden
not to be hoisted by just anyone Imagine
an open fire hose left in the hands

of a child *Don't say hate You should never
hate anybody* mothers warn us as they wipe
away grade school tears In the right
hands though At the right time though Hate

is the most useful tool A pressure
washer to strip out the deepest
stains The double jacket hose built
to knock down the hottest fires We have

no time left to value the valueless
Why struggle over the mountain when
we can blast through instead
Dynamite in the fissure The glory

of the boom Only the menopausal
can do it the way it should be done
Who else will cook the naughty
children Who else turns to salt

rather than never see home again
Tell me who when tied to the stake
laughs and laughs at the scratch
of the match It takes time to access

such tools Experience to wield them
well We tore down this ramshackle
house Let those of us on fire
burn its rubble to the ground

DON'T COME HOME

a-drinking Miss Loretta sang
with loving on your mind
Loretta wrote that song after
she and Patsy Cline became friends
Patsy taught Loretta how to move
what to say what to wear on stage
Taught her that the song not family
not love could structure her life
Told her she was the one
with the talent in that marriage
and it was time to quit taking
guff off of Doo No woman
knows how to woman until
she is taught No artist is an artist
unless she pleases first herself

The friendship between Patsy
and Loretta is at the core
of *Coal Miner's Daughter*
the rare movie made about
a woman singer It is the only movie
I stop to watch when I find it
on TV A movie that teaches
how to be the artist you are meant
to be when nobody says be that artist
A movie that shows what making
costs the maker

Sissy Spacek followed Loretta
around for a year to get ready
for that role Learned how
to sound like her walk like her
Sang with her on stage
at the Opry Two Lorettas
up there side by side If you made me
do an impersonation of Loretta Lynn
right now I would do *Patsy's always*
saying 'Little girl you got to run
your own life' But my life's running me
Me doing Spacek doing Loretta doing Patsy
So many knots in the string

When Loretta had twins
she named one Peggy and one Patsy
One after her sister One after Cline
When we moved to Georgia the first
friend my mother made was named
Peggy and I learned I should call her
Miss Peggy since she was a grownup
I knew through my parents Miss Peggy
had the slowest steepest accent ever
Tanya she would say when I saw her
and my name went tumbling
A rock falling down its own hill
You tell your momma I said hey
One afternoon at the Food Lion
I said hello to Miss Peggy in line
only to have her turn around
and give me a one arm squeeze

Hey Sugar I'm Patsy not Peggy
Looked the same Laughed the same
Talked the same Identical twins
Just like in a soap opera No two
people were ever more alike
Not Peggy and Patsy Lynn
Not Sissy Spacek and Miss Loretta
Not me and my mother

Soap operas are the best because
every day is a new chapter
in the longest story most of us
will ever know Characters might die
on a soap but seldom do they
stay dead Old actors return
with some cockamamie explanation
for their absence A new actor
steps in and everyone pretends
the character always looked
just like that

Miss Loretta died the other day
The Peggys and Patsys are gone too
Beulah and Edna and Edith and Mildred
all have moved along Which leaves me
Last of the knots End of the string
And never a stranger to meet

BUILD BACK BUTCH

by backwards born a baby By
build barber Build bar Build beer
belt boots Stiffen spine Stiffen
quiff Whiff of smoke Shift soil
Plant rows Come up monster

Volunteer tall in the field Stalk
amid bushes Corn among beans
Birds flee Hornworms shrink
Underneath earth rolls
Below wasps thrum

Still hair product Still beeswax
Still petroleum Necessary hair
to sky Friday tie Saturday denim
Chain of keys Pocket of change
Every bathroom a battleground

LET ME NOT FORGET ME NOT

Let me not be the last
lesbian who remembers
our bars Such smoky
bars Everyone smoking
Serious smokers Cocktail
smokers People smoking
outside People smoking
in Smoking Marlboro Reds
Camel Blues Smoking
American Spirit cigarillos
and cloves Waking to the reek
of stale smoke the first
reminder you had been out
the night before Let us
remember these sticky
bars For we drank and
drank and drinking spilled
Spilled Budweiser Spilled
Zima Spilled Jaeger
Spilled Slippery Nipples
Spilled Sex on the Beach
Spilled bottom shelf
tequila Spilled every rum
and coke I ever ordered
Spilled them on ourselves
Spilled them on each other
Fought over the spilling

Forgave each other
for spilling Drank because
bars were the place to look
Bars the place a trueself
shown Bars a place
the trueself seen Straight
people seldom in our bars
then Straight people with
better options than bars
with latenight stickyfloor
pushyshovey fights Fights
over love Love real Love
imagined Bouncer steps
in to break up the fight
Bouncer a bulldyke
in boots hat and tie
Hurrah hurrah for
these bars and dykes
Remember them
both forever

Let me not be the last lesbian
who found her people on a screen
Not the last to recognize herself
in the light butches of TV
Tatum Kristy Jodie Jo
Let me not be the last who
learned to crush through
the screen MaryAnn Lori Kelly
No one knows who you look
at when you watch TV No one

knows the way you see
Let every lesbian always
remember our long promised
Dusty Springfield biopic
Let us count the number
of gay boy biopics made
during those same years
Remember the annual rumor
of who this time would play her
KD Melissa Adele Nicole
Glory glory dykes and amazons
We must make them make
our movies

We must remember forever
Whitney and Robyn We
must never forget their love
Remember how Cissy
and the brothers tried
to make them hide their
love We heard the words
that screened their love
We saw through love's
tuneful disguise When
Whitney confesses *I get so
emotional baby every time
I think of you* we knew
who she was talking to
When Whitney states *Ain't
it shocking* what and then sits
for a moment in the heart

of that beat before she pivots
and drops the line back
in its track *what love*
can do we hear the name
that lives in the gap Whitney
dead now Dusty dead now
May we always hear the love
embedded in their soar

Let me not be the final
lesbian to believe
Dolly and Ann Richards
were a thing Not the last
to see them together
and recognize it as love
Dolly so solid in polkadots
and sequins Ann permanently
handsome in those Rose of Texas
boots Hurrah hurrah
for these stars and dykes
Stars and dykes forever

Let me not be the last butch
stranded on Last Butch Island
Let me not be the culminating
bulldagger Not the terminal
stud Not the concluding soft
butch Not the ultimate stone
Somebody has to bring an end
to the diesel dykes Someone
will be the final Butchie

McShorthair in town Surely
I can not be the last to wear
my hair like Elvis Not the
closing flattop Not the crowning
pompadour Let mine not be
the finale in a long line
of high and tights

If I am let me say I am sorry
Butches had a real chance
to make change and we blew it
We lived so far out we thought
getting in meant progress Lived
so far beyond we felt both diseased
and immune When they opened
the door right in the middle
of our kicking it down we took that
to mean we had won

And let us stop this story
before it goes any further
Butches are not being erased
Butches are not being replaced
It is simply our time to go

Extinct happens to everyone
Extinct just means swallowed
by the earth Extinct only says
someday diggers uncover
our bones Assistants turn up
buckles from our belts Tourists

buy commemorative keychains
Students sift for boot scraps
and wallets An intern designs
a sign for the site and queer
teens graffiti it the next day
A theorist speculates why we
played so much pool Some historian
earns tenure debating whether
80s butches were imagined or true
A museum installs a diorama
with too tall butches spread out
across a too bright bar Everyone
is frozen in a distinct moment of action
Smoking Drinking Gawking Lewd
It is shocking these far future
scientists will conclude
simply shocking
what love can do

AND THEY LOOK

alike too Like my mother and I
look alike Every time we see
Junior on *HeeHaw* she notes
He could be family Big moon
face Crinkle eye smile Family
is like a string to my mother
Every member a knot Connected
but apart *In heaven you will*
recognize every knot on our string
and they will already know you

One day my mother declares
she wants to be the woman
who sings backup and plays
tambourine for Culture Club
We have just gotten MTV
and still watch it like it is a show
Turn it on at the top of the hour
and sit there for 30 minutes
as the videos click by
Helen Terry I discover decades
later when we have the internet
and can wonder about a fact
and then find it My mother
long dead never searched the internet
My mother never sent an email
Helen Terry though is still alive

Helen Terry is the big voice
in all the great Culture Club songs
Karma Chameleon
I'll Tumble For You
I Know You Miss Me Blind
Hers is the voice that echoes
whatever Boy George sings first
I'm a man (a man)
without conviction
Hers is the voice that holds up his

Progress is seldom a true story
Step up Slide back But my friend
Clark always likes to point out
You and I would spend whole lunchtimes
discussing whether Boy George
might possibly be gay We share
pronouns at the start of meetings now
but honestly I do not want to tell you
my pronouns *Sirred* in line
Brothered by security *Hey guyed*
at the store These moments
of slippage are pure butch
triumph Between the guess
the confusion the correction
I feel most seen

I know how to watch MTV now
Know how to look up facts Have yet
to spend meaningful time with
my mother since she died Spotted

her in the highest row of a stadium
once She stood when I stood Sat
when I sat They call my name
and she pounds her hands together
like she is playing a tambourine
She shows up in my dreams but
we speak of nothing real I know not
of an afterlife or if we are gifted
some chance to live again In this
as in so many things I am a man
(a man) who does not know

UP MY TREE

he builds a place A place
just for me The stand a boat
a mountain a sea Under me

the branch that withstood
the lightning Under me pads
the mother cat From her mouth

hangs a kitten The kitten who
skittered from the pile A kitten
trying to leave From the mouth

of the kitten come monster
meows Meows made mostly
of *eees* Meows that come from

instinct Meows that will certainly
change As the kitten listens
the kitten will learn From siblings From

her mother From birds dogs and hogs
As the kitten listens to me *Me-ow*
I say to the kitten Two syllables Emphasis

on the *e* Mother drops the kitten
back in the sunshine pile Dreamers
wake Sleepers shift Paces her way

back under the tree Lifts her head Sniffs
old lightning Considers my book Licks
her whiskers Paws an apple Bites at a bee

And up grows the corn Up
grow the beans Up climbs
the mother Up grows me

HAVING REACHED
THE MIDDLE

(as if I could be that lucky)
I have forgotten ahead Look
only back Not a nostalgia
More a hard digging Uncover
Stitch together a story
that explains me to me
A young girl flies through
a field Her arms spin about
her like pinwheels Before her
birds rise A man teaches
her to drive She wants
to leave as he leaves Wants
to decide if and how
to return A woman shows
her how to patchwork sew
How to join together Make
something from what lies
at hand What are parents
but people People who bring
us up People who push us
under I come from

a long line of union and farmer
Democrats A disappearing
class rumored soon to be extinct
Am descended from a lineage

of women with names like
Edna Beulah Edith Mildred
Old-time names gone missing
from use I have lived on a farm
In big cities In small cities In suburbs
In small towns I hope I have
already been as poor as I ever
will be Been lower middle class
Working class Middle class
Worked hourly Salaried Parttime
Fulltime Been a temp Worked
legally Worked illegally Got paid
in bank accounts Under the table
Off the books Been a teacher College
Community college Highschool
University Made Mr Mistys Blizzards
Dipped cones Made Subway Clubs
and BMTs Worked production lines
Made movie cases Made ostomy supplies
Wafer Pouch Barrier Stoma Built
Poems Syllabi Assignments Lectures
Been shaped

by geography Midwest turned
South White migration
the Great Migration backwards
North to South Not fleeing
Still farm to city though Still
fewer chances to more Illinois
Georgia North Carolina Maryland
Impossible to imagine I might never

live South again If I die here
never again will I enjoy good BBQ
No more a meat and three No
river swims No giant bugs My
blood will grow thicker and thicker
I finally quit waving at strangers
Just stopped chatting at checkout
Don't ask how they are doing
Don't ask about their day Mash
my lips together Focus on standing
there quiet Unless I return South
I will never eat a decent biscuit
again After I came out

to my mother she wrote me
a letter explaining I could not
be a lesbian because I came
from a long line of strong
independent pioneer women
I thought perhaps she made
my point I walked in Dyke
Marches Pride Parades when
queers were the ones actually
marching Folks we passed
averted their eyes so as not
to shame us by seeing us
We thought perhaps they
missed our point Made signs
with markers and cardboard
Out Today Out To Stay

We Are Everywhere because
they claimed we did not exist
Same things said about
trans kids now Shift who
should feel shame and call it
progress Marches then
drew protesters Churches
and families huddled
on corners concerned about
Hell and Flames and Eternal
Souls We would Stop Circle
Point Chant *Be nice Be nice*
No one changed but we won
We won because we lasted
We won because we were right
Did you know Lesbian Avengers
started to eat fire after skinheads
torched a house full of queers
Lesbian Avengers drew bombs
on their flyers with the promise
We Recruit Lesbian Avengers
won when they walked back
into the burning room Won
because they swallowed the fire
The final Pride I attended was nothing
but corporation sponsored floats
throwing rainbow branded swag
at kids and queers who stood
on the sidewalk and clapped
PFLAG the only thing I love still

I tear up as they march wave hug
Mothers and fathers so willing
to love Drunks are fans of rules

and patterns Drunks love a circle
much more than most Live in them
drunk Sit in them sober Drinking
makes change feel impossible
What today is tomorrow is destined
to be But the truth is every person
has an ability to change Everyone
contains a chance to get better
Drunks believe everyone recovers
by walking the same path Drunks
recruit to show others
how to walk it too Do not
drink this second Do not drink
this minute Do not drink for an
hour Do not drink today Stitch
enough of this time together
and a brain will start to change
Drunks know every sober minute
is a miracle Drunks drink because
they believe they are special Drunks
drink because they are sure they feel
see suffer more than anyone else alive
Drunks love sayings because wet
brains struggle to think reason decide
I got better when I learned to feel
my feelings instead of drown them
in a glass I got better when I saw myself

as human not monster I became
a better poet a better teacher
from the repetition of sobriety
Say a thought one way Then say it
again another Having reached
the middle (late middle)

I want to tell myself a story
Put myself to sleep A girl begins
to read Reads her way away
A girl learns to drive Drives
her way away A girl is taught
to make do with what lies
at hand So she gathers her things
and builds a path away Sometimes
she wonders if she would be
the same person if she had stayed
Frankenstein becomes a favorite novel
She reads it again and again
We say Frankenstein to mean
both monster and maker We forget
Frankenstein is written by a woman
whose mother died
because she was born
The story tells of a creation
that tries to destroy its creator
The book ends when the monster
vows to leave the one who made him
The girl loves the middle part best
Where the hunter and the hunted
switch roles

NOTES

Born Backwards refers briefly to *Return to Sender*, a song recorded by Elvis Presley in 1962 and written by Otis Blackwell and Winfield Scott; *Frankenstein: or, The Modern Prometheus*, an 1818 novel by Mary Shelley; and *The Song of the Wandering Aengus*, a poem by W.B. Yeats, published in 1899

What A Poem Do refers briefly to *I'm Thinking Tonight of my Blue Eyes* and *You Are My Flower*, both traditional songs, reworked and covered by The Carter Family

Poet Is Pig contains lines from *Root Hog or Die*. There are many versions of songs with this title; the poem refers to the one performed by June Carter Cash

Karma Police contains lines from *The Storms Are On The Ocean*, an old Scottish ballad; the poem refers to the version recorded by The Carter Family

And They Look contains lines from *Karma Chameleon*, a 1983 song written and performed by Culture Club

Don't Come Home refers briefly to *Don't Come Home A-Drinkin'*, a song written by Loretta Lynn and her sister, Peggy Sue Wright in 1967. The poem also references *Coal Miner's Daughter*, a film based on Loretta Lynn's 1976 autobiography of the same name. The film was directed by Michael Apted and released in 1980

Let Me Not contains lines from *So Emotional*, a song most notably recorded by Whitney Houston in 1987, written by Billy Stenberg and Tom Kelly. The poem also references *Stars and Dykes Forever*, a work of art made by Delia Davis in 1973.

These poems appeared in the following sites, often in earlier versions. Thanks to the editors who gave them a home.

Sinister Wisdom: Common Lives/Lesbian Lives. *Let Me Not Forget Me Not* and *Having Reached The Middle*. February 2025

DC Queer Pride Poem-A-Day. Video. *And They Look*. June 2024

DC Queer Pride Poem-A-Day. Video. *Born Backwards*. June 2023

Smartish Pace. *Don't Come Home* and *We The Menopausal*. April 2023

DC Queer Pride Poem-A-Day. Video. *Let Me Not*. June 2022

Metro Weekly. *Build Back Butch*. June 2022

ACKNOWLEDGMENTS

Endless gratitude to the entire YesYes Books team, especially publisher KMA Sullivan. Her editorial work on this book made it better again and again; her support of poets and poetry is heroic. Thanks as well to designer Alban Fisher, whose visual choices always thrill.

Much appreciation to the Arts Club of Washington for hosting a residency for queer DMV-area poets. Making a space for such a community helped this book find itself.

Admiration as well to the members of the Arts Club 5 (Kim Robinson, Sunu Chandy, Dan Vera, Malik Thompson) for their feedback on many of these poems and sharing their own work with me. Their thoughtfulness and artistry made this a better book.

Special love goes out, as it does every day, to Susan Pietrzyk. Her steady support makes this book possible. Anywhere these poems argue for love or connection is directly shaped by her presence.

Finally, this book is built from the deep love, admiration, and gratitude I hold for both my parents, Gerald Milton Olson (1938–2014) and Mildred Ann Campbell Olson (1943–1995). I love and miss them every day.

ALSO FROM YESYES BOOKS

www.ingramcontent.com/pod-product-compliance
Lightning Source LLC
Chambersburg PA
CBHW050844270326
41930CB00020B/3475